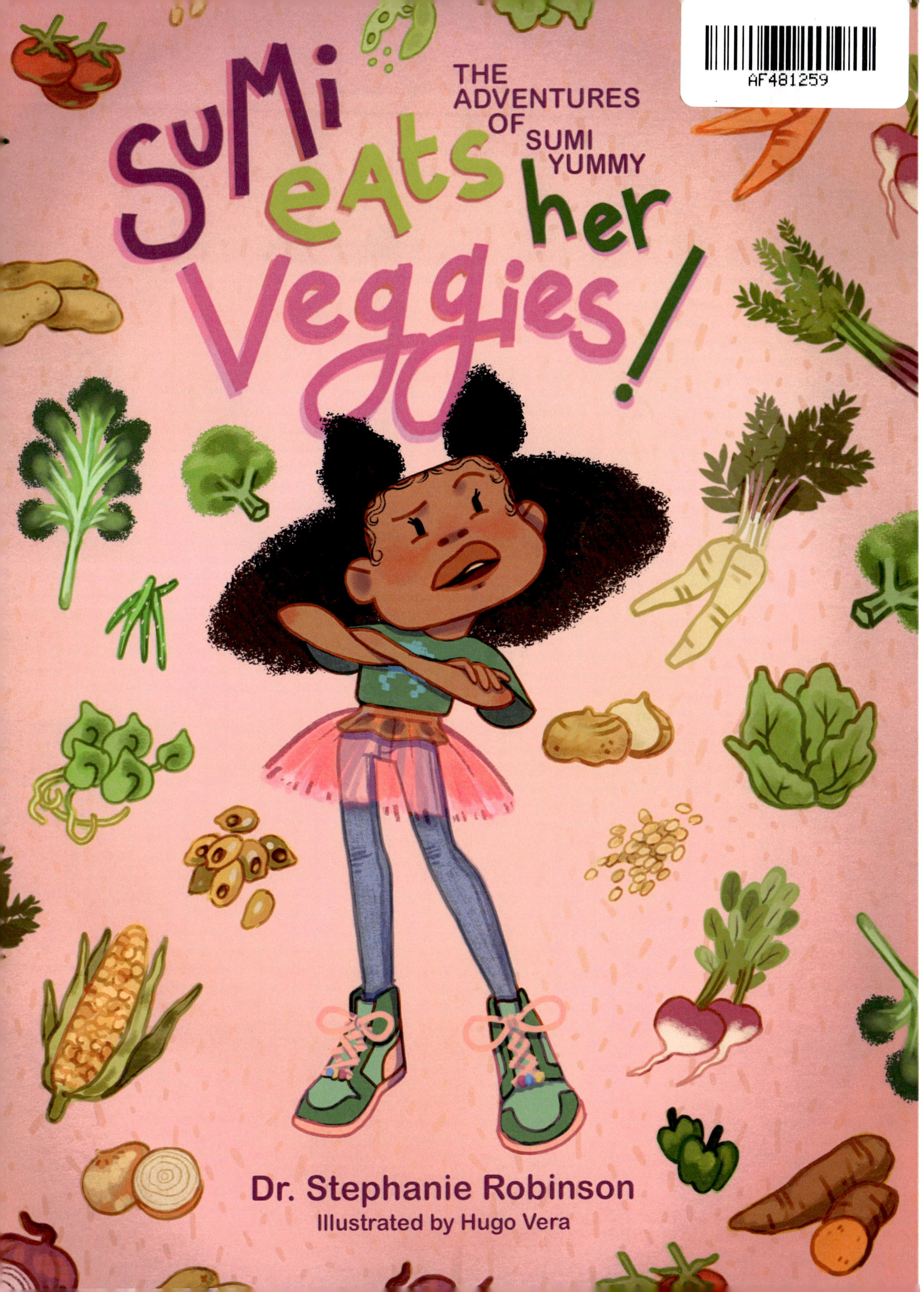

SUMI EATS her Veggies!
THE ADVENTURES OF SUMI YUMMY
Dr. Stephanie Robinson
Illustrated by Hugo Vera
AF481259

Once upon a time in Veggie Land,
Sumi Yummy refused to eat her veggies.

Mrs. Yummy tried everything to get
Sumi to eat her veggies.

But, Sumi still refused.

Then a light bulb went off
in Mrs. Yummy's head.

Sumi loved hamburgers.

One day Mrs. Yummy made a broccoli burger because Sumi loves broccoli.

Mrs. Yummy put the burger on the table
with sweet potato fries.

Sumi took one small bite and smiled.
She loved her veggie burger and fries!

Every burger had a "secret" ingredient of a different veggie.

Every day Mrs. Yummy made different burgers using her "secret" veggie recipe.

Sumi ate broccoli burgers, eggplant burgers, zucchini burgers, dandelion burgers.

Sumi loves eating her veggie burgers.

SUMI YUMMY VEGGIE BURGER RECIPE

Sumi helps her mom make and cook veggie burgers. You can do the same! Add your favorite vegetables and make a delicious, nutritious, and healthy-eating veggie burger!

Ingredients:

2 Eggs – Binder to hold burger patties together
Your favorite veggie - 2/3 cup
Your favorite veggie - 2/3 cup
Your favorite veggie -2/3/cup
Parsley leaves - 1/4 cup
Corn flour - 2-4 Tbsp
1-16 oz. can of Black Beans {rinse and drain} (optional)
Salt to taste

Pre-heat oven to 180

Recipe:
Place veggies in a blender or food processor; pulse until coarsely chopped.
Transfer to a large bowl.
Add eggs to the veggie mix – stir and mix
Add salt to taste
Add 2-4 tbsp corn flour – stir and mix
Line baking pan with parchment paper
Scoop a tablespoon of mix onto parchment paper

(Can make up to 6 veggie burgers)

Place into oven and bake at 180 degrees until slightly brown (10-15 minutes)

Flip burgers onto the other side

Bake until slightly brown (10-15 minutes)

Remove from baking pan; turn off oven

Put veggie burgers onto a dish

Serve (can use hamburger buns to create a veggie burger sandwich with condiments).

YUMMY!

 # SUMI YUMMY VEGGIE TASTING ACTIVITY

LEARNING OBJECTIVE:

The activity will help children increase their awareness, knowledge, and exploration of various vegetables, taste differences, and textures.

WHAT YOU WILL NEED-VEGETABLES/OBJECTS

Have children explore different vegetables by placing vegetables on table. The vegetables can be cut into smaller chunks for children to taste test.

ACTIVITY

- *Have children use their senses to smell, touch, and taste vegetables.*
- *Discuss the differences and similarities between the vegetables' smell, taste, and touch.*
- *Have children write down which vegetables they like and did not like. The information can be useful when making veggie burgers.*

SUMI YUMMY PLANTS A VEGETABLE GARDEN ACTIVITY

LEARNING OBJECTIVE:

Have children learn the importance of where vegetables come from, and how they grow. The activity will help children learn patience by watching a plant grow from a seed to a plant. It will teach them responsibility by having them create a schedule on a calendar when to water the plants and feed it nutrients (plant food). The children will learn to stay focused and calm when caring for their plant(s). They will learn the importance of reaping what they sow.

WHAT YOU WILL NEED

- *Vegetable seeds/or pre-planted vegetable plants in planters.*
- *Soil/Dirt*
- *A location to plant veggies or pre-planted plants*
- *Planter box(es)*
- *A calendar*

ACTIVITY

- *Have children place seeds into a layer of dirt placed into the planter box(es); or the pre-planted plants.*
- *Have children follow care instructions relating to watering plants, soil/dirt to use, and required sunlight.*
- *Have children mark on the calendar when the seeds begin to sprout; or when the plants can to grow.*

Vegetables A-Z

flower
Celeriac
Celery
Chard (Red and Swiss)
Chicory
Cress
Cucumbers
Daikon
Garlic
n Beans
Greens
Collard Greens
Mustard Greens
Gourds

Jicama
Kale
Kohlrabi
Leeks
Arugula Lettuce
Butter Lettuce
Endive Lettuce
Green and Red Leaf Lettuce
Romaine Lettuce
Lima Beans
Mushrooms
Okra
Onions
Green Onions
Parsnips

Snap Sugar Peas
Snow Peas
Anaheim Peppers
Sweet peppers
oes
Pumpkin
Radicchio
Radish
Rhubarb
anesco (cauliflower)
Rutabaga
Shallots
Spinach
Squash

Acorn Squash	Butternut Squash	Patti Pan Squash	Spaghetti Squash	Swede
Sweet Potato	Tomatillo	Tomatoes	Turnips	Water Chestnuts
Yam	Zucchini